LUTHER'S SMALL CATECHISM

Study Edition

Augsburg Fortress
Minneapolis

LUTHER'S SMALL CATECHISM
with *Evangelical Lutheran Worship* texts
Study Edition

Copyright © 2008 Augsburg Fortress, Publishers
All rights reserved.

Original copyright © 1994, 2000 Augsburg Fortress, Publishers
Introduction and translation by Timothy J. Wengert

Robert Buckley Farlee and Andrew De Young, editors
Nicholas Markell, Markell Studios, liturgical artist

Scripture quotations are from New Revised Standard Version Bible, copyright
© 1989 Division of Christian Education of the National Council of the
Churches of Christ in the United States of America. Used by permission.

The following is reprinted from *Evangelical Lutheran Worship*, copyright © 2006:
Individual Confession and Forgiveness; Holy Communion words of institution; the Marriage service; the service of Holy Baptism.

The English translations of the Lord's Prayer and the Apostles' Creed are prepared by the English Language Liturgical Consultation, copyright © 1988.

Quotations from *Luther's Works* Vol. 50 copyright © 1975 Fortress Press and
Vol. 51 copyright © 1959 Fortress Press.

This book was typeset using Adobe Jenson MM, Metron, and Requiem.

The paper used in this publication meets the minimum requirements of
American National Standard for Information Sciences—Permanence of
Paper for Printed Materials, ANSI Z329.48-1984.

Manufactured in the U.S.A.   ISBN 978-0-8066-5605-2

18 17 16 15 14 13 12 11 10 09 08   1 2 3 4 5 6 7 8 9 10

Presented to

_____

by

_____

on

_____

CONTENTS

HOW TO USE THIS BOOK

This introduction to the Small Catechism has three parts: "Where Do Catechisms Come From?" "What Martin Luther Added to the Catechism," and "Ways to Use this Book."

WHERE DO CATECHISMS COME FROM?

In 1529 Martin Luther, a pastor in the German town of Wittenberg and teacher at the university there, published his explanations to the chief parts of the Christian faith. These explanations were first produced on individual sheets and sold for a few pennies each. By the middle of 1529 printers in Wittenberg and elsewhere had collected them into what they called an *enchiridion* or handbook. Luther added a preface, which told pastors how to use the book, and he also attached several other sections to the end of it. By the end of the year printers had given this handbook a subtitle by which we know it today, *The Small Catechism of Martin Luther*. They

gave it this name because in the same year Luther published a set of his sermons on the same topics. This book of sermons, then called *The German Catechism*, is now known as the Large Catechism.

But the term *catechism* is much older than Luther's work from 1529. It comes from the Greek *kata-echo*, which means "to repeat back." Already by the year

A.D. 400, Latin-speaking Christians used the word *catechism* to describe the basic instruction given to new Christians. As they learned, they recited the things they heard from their teachers. By the Middle Ages *catechism* had come to mean the three things that all Christians should know: the Ten Commandments, the Apostles' Creed, and the Lord's Prayer. By the time Martin Luther was growing up in central Europe during the 1490s, pastors were required to teach these three things to all adults and children and to preach on them during weekday services four times a year. When Luther became an assistant preacher in 1514, he preached on these three chief parts. Some of his sermons were copied down and published. In 1528, during the absence of Wittenberg's head pastor, John Bugenhagen, Luther preached again on the three chief parts. The Small and Large Catechisms came from these sermons.

WHAT MARTIN LUTHER ADDED TO THE CATECHISM

As Martin Luther was teaching these three chief parts to children and adults in Wittenberg, he added some things that his own congregation probably thought of as very new. In fact, these new parts go back to the very beginning of Christianity and the good news of Jesus' death and resurrection. Combined with the original catechism, these additions have helped people from Luther's day right down to our own times hear and understand the heart of the Christian faith. Learning what Luther added to the three chief parts of the early catechism may help you use this book well.

1. Two "New" Chief Parts

As the table of contents shows, to the original three chief parts of the catechism Martin Luther added two more: explanations of Holy Baptism and Holy Communion. We often call them sacraments, or visible words of God, because they combine physical elements with God's command and promise. Here God comes to us in very personal ways: combining God's name and ours in baptism and feeding our bodies with Christ's body and blood in the Lord's supper. By including these sacraments—the visible words—with God's spoken word in the Ten Commandments, Apostles' Creed, and Lord's Prayer, Martin Luther reminds us that Christianity is not just about memorizing rules or doctrines or prayers, but that it focuses on what God does for us in Jesus Christ.

When Christians were asked in Luther's day to define the church, they responded that the church is not so much a building or an organization but an event that the Holy Spirit brings into being wherever the word of God is preached and the sacraments are administered to call and gather believers. By including the sacraments in the Small Catechism, Luther defines church for everyone who uses this book. Here God is at work making us believers.

2. The "New" Order

Many of the popular catechetical booklets published before Luther's Small Catechism emphasized what we must do to avoid God's anger and earn God's favor. Many times we may also think that God and Christianity are only about rules and regulations. The order of the Small Catechism helps correct that misunderstanding and focuses our attention on God's gifts to us. Luther insisted that Christians begin with the Ten Commandments, which show us God's demands and our inability to fulfill them, and then move to the Apostles' Creed, which declares what God does for us, and then to the Lord's Prayer, which teaches us where we may go for help.

The sacraments, too, give us what we need most from God: forgiveness of sins, life, and salvation. Thus, mirroring baptism, the Small Catechism moves from the "drowning" of the old person and our sins to the raising up of the new in faith.

One time Martin Luther reflected on this order and said that it was like a physician who begins with the diagnosis (the Ten Commandments) before offering treatment (the good news in the Apostles' Creed and Lord's Prayer). The point of the Small Catechism is to give us comfort and support when we face problems in our Christian life. At least that is what Katherine Luther, Martin Luther's wife, once said. In a letter to her near the end of his life, Martin Luther tried to calm her worries about his health by reminding her, "You, dear Katie, read [my sermons on the Gospel of] John and the Small Catechism, about which you once said: 'Everything in this book has been said about me.' For you prefer to worry about me instead of letting God worry" (*Luther's Works*, 50:302).

3. *The Question*

Other pastors in Martin Luther's day wrote catechisms with many complicated questions and answers. Luther's Small Catechism sticks for the most part to one simple question: "What is this?" (As an alternative, this edition includes the familiar expansion of this basic question, "What does this mean?") In fact, Luther is not so much interested in the deeper, hidden meanings of these chief parts as in basic definitions, such as "What is the First Commandment? or Amen? or Baptism?"

Luther used this simple question because he had found it effective when teaching Wittenberg's young people the catechism in his sermons. In 1529 he also had another inspiration for using such a simple question. Although he was forty-five years old, he had been a father for only three years. At that time little Hans Luther was running around the house pointing at everything and asking his father, "*Was ist das?*" ("What is this?"). His father used Hans' question in the Small Catechism.

4. *Luther's Faith*

This brings us to another important contribution in Martin Luther's little book. Most of the time when we learn the Small Catechism, the teacher asks the question and the student gives the answer. But when Luther was writing this material, he also was answering the questions many Christians were asking him: "What is this? How does this happen?" Thus, the Small Catechism is Martin Luther's confession of faith in God. In it, Luther tells us what these things are for him and for us.

You may discover that not only is Luther asking, "What is this?" but God also is asking. As you study the Small Catechism, you, too, are invited to confess, "God has created me; Jesus is my Lord; the Holy Spirit calls me and gathers me into the church."

5. The Center

The center of Martin Luther's confession of faith in the Small Catechism is the Apostles' Creed—that is, faith in God's promises. And the center of the Creed is God our creator, who, in the death and resurrection of Jesus Christ, rescues us from all evil. By the Holy Spirit God creates and strengthens our faith in Christ and his forgiveness. God's commandments, grounded in the First Commandment, show how much we need faith to "fear, love, and trust God." The Lord's Prayer is anchored by our heavenly Father's promise to listen and to act. The sacraments proclaim forgiveness and rescue in Jesus Christ.

WAYS TO USE THIS BOOK

Before Martin Luther's death in 1546 and certainly after that time, the Small Catechism became more and more simply a textbook for young students to memorize and recite. Some parts were omitted, others tacked on. Whole books were written explaining Luther's explanations! The Small Catechism presented here follows Luther's original concept more closely and allows us to use this book both in and outside the classroom. Here are some suggestions for use.

1. Handbook for the Household

When each individual part of the Small Catechism was sold separately, each sheet had this heading: ". . . in a simple way in which the head of a house is to present them to the household." In a sermon delivered in November, 1528, Luther addresses the fathers and mothers by saying, "Every father of a family is a bishop in his house and the wife a bishopess. Therefore remember that you in your homes are to help us carry on the ministry as we do in the church. If we do this we shall have a gracious God, who will defend us from all evil and in all evil" (*Luther's Works*, 51:137). Luther wrote the Small Catechism for the home, so that parents could explain to their children in simple terms the most important things in the Christian faith. For Luther the household is a house church.

Several additions to the Small Catechism underscore Luther's concern. There are sections for morning and evening prayers and for prayers before and after mealtimes. There is an entire section titled "The Household Chart of Some Bible Passages" (formerly called "Table of Duties"), in which Luther uses Bible verses to describe how we are to behave toward one another as parents, children, married people, workers, and the like. Also included in all booklet versions of the Small Catechism during Luther's lifetime and beyond were the services of Marriage and Holy Baptism: marriage because most households in Luther's day came into being at the time of marriage; baptism because that begins the life of faith for all Christians.

We can continue to use these things in our homes today. You can add Luther's table prayers to the ones your family may already be using. If you are not accustomed to praying in the morning or evening, Luther's brief prayers can strengthen your faith. The Bible passages Luther collected are only a few of the many that describe how Christ frees a Christian in faith toward God and love for one another. In this edition Luther's own prefaces to the Marriage and Baptism services appear, but the orders of worship have been replaced with material from today's *Evangelical Lutheran Worship*.

2. Prayer Book

One of the first ways Martin Luther taught people about the catechism was through prayer. Luther included suggestions for prayers in the morning and evening and at meals. Many of these prayers are from prayers written before Luther's time.

There are three ways to use the Small Catechism for prayer. First, you can use the prayers he suggests in your own personal or family devotions. Second, you can use the explanations of the Lord's Prayer to help you understand what we ask God for in that prayer. Third, you can actually use the various parts of the Small Catechism as the basis for your own prayers. Martin Luther described how he himself prayed the Ten Commandments, Apostles' Creed, and Lord's Prayer in a published letter written to his barber, Master Peter, who had asked him how to pray. Each commandment, article of the Creed, or petition of the Lord's Prayer suggests things we can request from God or thank God for receiving.

3. Worship Book

Along with the prayers, many early editions of the Small Catechism also included parts of the worship service to encourage worship in the household and the congregation. We have included the services of Holy Baptism, Marriage, and Individual Confession and Forgiveness. The five chief parts of the Small Catechism also have their place in worship. The Ten Commandments and Confession prepare us for Confession and Forgiveness. The Apostles' Creed and Lord's Prayer are used in many worship services. Holy Baptism and Holy Communion are two of the things that create the Christian church and gather it in worship around God's forgiveness in Jesus Christ.

The various parts of the Small Catechism also help us listen to the scripture readings and the sermon, since almost all of them will relate to one section of the catechism or another. The better we know the Small Catechism, the easier it will be to understand and hear God's word in the readings and preaching. As you listen, ask yourself, "What part of the catechism is this?"

4. A Key to the Bible

Few people realize that the original printings of the Small Catechism included artwork. There was one illustration based on a story from the

Bible for each commandment, article of the Creed, petition of the Lord's Prayer, and sacrament. The illustrations in Luther's day were woodcuts. Within 100 years this feature of the Small Catechism had nearly disappeared. In this book, however, we have once again introduced pictures. Many of the illustrations are based on the Bible stories selected for the Small Catechism published in Wittenberg in 1536. You will find a reference to the Bible under each illustration. Take time to look up these passages. As you do, you will learn more about some of the stories in the Bible.

May this little book open up the Bible to you and strengthen your faith!

Timothy J. Wengert
Philadelphia, Pennsylvania

Note to the reader:
There are other translations of the Small Catechism your congregation may also be using. This translation is based primarily on the edition of Luther's Small Catechism published at Wittenberg in 1536, in consultation with other authorial editions. It is part of a larger translation that appears in an edition of *The Book of Concord* (Minneapolis: Fortress Press, 2000). That edition includes many more historical notes for pastors and teachers.

THE TEN COMMANDMENTS

You shall have no other gods.
   I, the Lord your God, am a jealous God, punishing children for the iniquity of parents to the third and the fourth generation of those who reject me, but showing steadfast love to the thousandth generation of those who love me and keep my commandments.

You shall not make wrongful use
   of the name of the Lord your God.

Remember the sabbath day, and keep it holy.

Honor your father and your mother.

You shall not murder.

You shall not commit adultery.

You shall not steal.

You shall not bear false witness against your neighbor.

You shall not covet your neighbor's house.

You shall not covet your neighbor's wife,
   or male or female slave, or ox, or donkey,
   or anything that belongs to your neighbor.

from Exodus 20:1-17

THE FIRST COMMANDMENT

You shall have no other gods.

WHAT IS THIS? *or* **WHAT DOES THIS MEAN?**

We are to fear, love, and trust God above all things.

from Exodus 32

THE SECOND COMMANDMENT

You shall not make wrongful use of the name of the Lord your God.

WHAT IS THIS? *or* **WHAT DOES THIS MEAN?**

We are to fear and love God, so that we do not curse, swear, practice magic, lie, or deceive using God's name, but instead use that very name in every time of need to call on, pray to, praise, and give thanks to God.

from Leviticus 24:10-16

THE THIRD COMMANDMENT

Remember the sabbath day, and keep it holy.

WHAT IS THIS? *or* **WHAT DOES THIS MEAN?**

We are to fear and love God, so that we do not despise preaching or God's word, but instead keep that word holy and gladly hear and learn it.

from Luke 10:38-42

THE FOURTH COMMANDMENT

Honor your father and your mother.

WHAT IS THIS? *or* **WHAT DOES THIS MEAN?**

We are to fear and love God, so that we neither despise nor anger our parents and others in authority, but instead honor, serve, obey, love, and respect them.

from Luke 2:41-52

THE FIFTH COMMANDMENT

You shall not murder.

WHAT IS THIS? *or* **WHAT DOES THIS MEAN?**

We are to fear and love God, so that we neither endanger nor harm the lives of our neighbors, but instead help and support them in all of life's needs.

from Genesis 4:1-16

THE SIXTH COMMANDMENT

You shall not commit adultery.

WHAT IS THIS? *or* **WHAT DOES THIS MEAN?**

We are to fear and love God, so that we lead pure and decent lives in word and deed, and each of us loves and honors his or her spouse.

from 2 Samuel 11

THE SEVENTH COMMANDMENT

You shall not steal.

WHAT IS THIS? *or* **WHAT DOES THIS MEAN?**

We are to fear and love God, so that we neither take our neighbors' money or property nor acquire them by using shoddy merchandise or crooked deals, but instead help them to improve and protect their property and income.

from Joshua 7:1

THE EIGHTH COMMANDMENT

You shall not bear false witness against your neighbor.

WHAT IS THIS? *or* **WHAT DOES THIS MEAN?**

We are to fear and love God, so that we do not tell lies about our neighbors, betray or slander them, or destroy their reputations. Instead we are to come to their defense, speak well of them, and interpret everything they do in the best possible light.

from Luke 22:54-62

THE NINTH COMMANDMENT

You shall not covet your neighbor's house.

WHAT IS THIS? *or* **WHAT DOES THIS MEAN?**

We are to fear and love God, so that we do not try to trick our neighbors out of their inheritance or property or try to get it for ourselves by claiming to have a legal right to it and the like, but instead be of help and service to them in keeping what is theirs.

THE TENTH COMMANDMENT

You shall not covet your neighbor's wife, or male or female slave, or ox, or donkey, or anything that belongs to your neighbor.

WHAT IS THIS? *or* **WHAT DOES THIS MEAN?**

We are to fear and love God, so that we do not entice, force, or steal away from our neighbors their spouses, household workers, or livestock, but instead urge them to stay and fulfill their responsibilities to our neighbors.

CONCLUSION

WHAT THEN DOES GOD SAY ABOUT ALL THESE COMMANDMENTS?

God says the following: "I, the Lord your God, am a jealous God, punishing children for the iniquity of parents, to the third and the fourth generation of those who reject me, but showing steadfast love to the thousandth generation of those who love me and keep my commandments."

WHAT IS THIS? *or* **WHAT DOES THIS MEAN?**

God threatens to punish all who break these commandments. Therefore we are to fear his wrath and not disobey these commandments. However, God promises grace and every good thing to all those who keep these commandments. Therefore we also are to love and trust him and gladly act according to his commands.

THE APOSTLES' CREED

I believe in God, the Father almighty,
    creator of heaven and earth.

I believe in Jesus Christ, God's only Son, our Lord,
    who was conceived by the Holy Spirit,
    born of the virgin Mary,
    suffered under Pontius Pilate,
    was crucified, died, and was buried;
    he descended to the dead.*
    On the third day he rose again;
    he ascended into heaven,
    he is seated at the right hand of the Father,
    and he will come to judge the living and the dead.

I believe in the Holy Spirit,
    the holy catholic church,
    the communion of saints,
    the forgiveness of sins,
    the resurrection of the body,
    and the life everlasting. Amen.

* Or, "he descended into hell," another translation of this text in widespread use.

from Psalm 8

THE FIRST ARTICLE:
ON CREATION

I believe in God, the Father almighty,
    creator of heaven and earth.

WHAT IS THIS? *or* WHAT DOES THIS MEAN?

I believe that God has created me together with all that exists. God has given me and still preserves my body and soul: eyes, ears, and all limbs and senses; reason and all mental faculties.

In addition, God daily and abundantly provides shoes and clothing, food and drink, house and farm, spouse and children, fields, livestock, and all property—along with all the necessities and nourishment for this body and life. God protects me against all danger and shields and preserves me from all evil. And all this is done out of pure, fatherly, and divine goodness and mercy, without any merit or worthiness of mine at all! For all of this I owe it to God to thank and praise, serve and obey him. This is most certainly true.

from Luke 23:39-46

THE SECOND ARTICLE:
ON REDEMPTION

I believe in Jesus Christ, God's only Son, our Lord,
 who was conceived by the Holy Spirit,
 born of the virgin Mary,
 suffered under Pontius Pilate,
 was crucified, died, and was buried;
 he descended to the dead.
 On the third day he rose again;
 he ascended into heaven,
 he is seated at the right hand of the Father,
 and he will come to judge the living and the dead.

WHAT IS THIS? *or* WHAT DOES THIS MEAN?

I believe that Jesus Christ, true God, begotten of the Father in eternity, and also a true human being, born of the virgin Mary, is my Lord. He has redeemed me, a lost and condemned human being. He has purchased and freed me from all sins, from death, and from the power of the devil, not with gold or silver but with his holy, precious blood and with his innocent suffering and death. He has done all this in order that I may belong to him, live under him in his kingdom, and serve him in eternal righteousness, innocence, and blessedness, just as he is risen from the dead and lives and rules eternally. This is most certainly true.

from Acts 2

THE THIRD ARTICLE:
ON BEING MADE HOLY

I believe in the Holy Spirit,
>   the holy catholic church,
>   the communion of saints,
>   the forgiveness of sins,
>   the resurrection of the body,
>   and the life everlasting. Amen.

WHAT IS THIS? *or* **WHAT DOES THIS MEAN?**

I believe that by my own understanding or strength I cannot believe in Jesus Christ my Lord or come to him, but instead the Holy Spirit has called me through the gospel, enlightened me with his gifts, made me holy and kept me in the true faith, just as he calls, gathers, enlightens, and makes holy the whole Christian church on earth and keeps it with Jesus Christ in the one common, true faith. Daily in this Christian church the Holy Spirit abundantly forgives all sins—mine and those of all believers. On the last day the Holy Spirit will raise me and all the dead and will give to me and all believers in Christ eternal life. This is most certainly true.

from Mark 14:32-42

THE LORD'S PRAYER

Our Father in heaven,
   hallowed be your name,
   your kingdom come,
   your will be done, on earth as in heaven.
Give us today our daily bread.
Forgive us our sins
   as we forgive those who sin against us.
Save us from the time of trial
   and deliver us from evil.
For the kingdom, the power, and the glory are yours,
   now and forever. Amen.

Our Father, who art in heaven,
   hallowed be thy name,
   thy kingdom come,
   thy will be done, on earth as it is in heaven.
Give us this day our daily bread;
and forgive us our trespasses,
   as we forgive those who trespass against us;
and lead us not into temptation,
   but deliver us from evil.
For thine is the kingdom, and the power, and the glory,
   forever and ever. Amen.

INTRODUCTION

Our Father in heaven.

WHAT IS THIS? *or* **WHAT DOES THIS MEAN?**

With these words God wants to attract us, so that we come to believe he is truly our Father and we are truly his children, in order that we may ask him boldly and with complete confidence, just as loving children ask their loving father.*

THE FIRST PETITION**

Hallowed be your name.

WHAT IS THIS? *or* **WHAT DOES THIS MEAN?**

It is true that God's name is holy in itself, but we ask in this prayer that it may also become holy in and among us.

---

* Luther added this explanation to the Small Catechism in 1531 when his oldest child was five years old.

** The word petition means "request."

HOW DOES THIS COME ABOUT?

Whenever the word of God is taught clearly and purely and we, as God's children, also live holy lives according to it. To this end help us, dear Father in heaven! However, whoever teaches and lives otherwise than the word of God teaches, dishonors the name of God among us. Preserve us from this, heavenly Father!

from Acts 13:13-47

THE SECOND PETITION

Your kingdom come.

WHAT IS THIS? *or* **WHAT DOES THIS MEAN?**

In fact, God's kingdom comes on its own without our prayer, but we ask in this prayer that it may also come to us.

HOW DOES THIS COME ABOUT?

Whenever our heavenly Father gives us his Holy Spirit, so that through the Holy Spirit's grace we believe God's holy word and live godly lives here in time and hereafter in eternity.

from Luke 15:8-10

THE THIRD PETITION

Your will be done, on earth as in heaven.

WHAT IS THIS? *or* WHAT DOES THIS MEAN?

In fact, God's good and gracious will comes about without our prayer, but we ask in this prayer that it may also come about in and among us.

HOW DOES THIS COME ABOUT?

Whenever God breaks and hinders every evil scheme and will—as are present in the will of the devil, the world, and our flesh—that would not allow us to hallow God's name and would prevent the coming of his kingdom, and instead whenever God strengthens us and keeps us steadfast in his word and in faith until the end of our lives. This is God's gracious and good will.

from Matthew 27:27-31

37

THE FOURTH PETITION

Give us today our daily bread.

WHAT IS THIS? *or* WHAT DOES THIS MEAN?

In fact, God gives daily bread without our prayer, even to all evil people, but we ask in this prayer that God cause us to recognize what our daily bread is and to receive it with thanksgiving.

WHAT THEN DOES "DAILY BREAD" MEAN?

Everything included in the necessities and nourishment for our bodies, such as food, drink, clothing, shoes, house, farm, fields, livestock, money, property, an upright spouse, upright children, upright members of the household, upright and faithful rulers, good government, good weather, peace, health, decency, honor, good friends, faithful neighbors, and the like.

from John 6:8-10

THE FIFTH PETITION

Forgive us our sins
as we forgive those who sin against us.

WHAT IS THIS? *or* **WHAT DOES THIS MEAN?**

We ask in this prayer that our heavenly Father would not regard our sins nor deny these petitions on their account, for we are worthy of nothing for which we ask, nor have we earned it. Instead we ask that God would give us all things by grace, for we sin daily and indeed deserve only punishment. So, on the other hand, we, too, truly want to forgive heartily and to do good gladly to those who sin against us.

from Matthew 18:23-35

THE SIXTH PETITION

Save us from the time of trial.

WHAT IS THIS? *or* **WHAT DOES THIS MEAN?**

It is true that God tempts no one, but we ask in this prayer that God would preserve and keep us, so that the devil, the world, and our flesh may not deceive us or mislead us into false belief, despair, and other great and shameful sins, and that, although we may be attacked by them, we may finally prevail and gain the victory.

from Matthew 4:4-11

THE SEVENTH PETITION

And deliver us from evil.

WHAT IS THIS? *or* **WHAT DOES THIS MEAN?**

We ask in this prayer, as in a summary, that our Father in heaven may deliver us from all kinds of evil—affecting body or soul, property or reputation—and at last, when our final hour comes, may grant us a blessed end and take us by grace from this valley of tears to himself in heaven.

from Matthew 15:21-28

41

CONCLUSION

For the kingdom, the power, and the glory are yours,
now and forever.*
Amen.

WHAT IS THIS? *or* **WHAT DOES THIS MEAN?**

That I should be certain that such petitions are acceptable to and heard by our Father in heaven, for God himself commanded us to pray like this and has promised to hear us. "Amen, amen" means "Yes, yes, it is going to come about just like this."

---

* Some later editions of the catechism, printed after Luther's death, add this conclusion, commonly called the Doxology. Although found in Erasmus's editions of the Greek New Testament and in Luther's translation of that into German, Luther himself consistently followed the medieval practice and omitted it. The question and answer refer to "Amen."

1. WHAT IS BAPTISM?

Baptism is not simply plain water. Instead, it is water used according to God's command and connected with God's word.

WHAT THEN IS THIS WORD OF GOD?

Where our Lord Jesus Christ says in Matthew 28, "Go therefore and make disciples of all nations, baptizing them in the name of the Father and of the Son and of the Holy Spirit."

2. WHAT GIFTS or BENEFITS DOES BAPTISM GRANT?

It brings about forgiveness of sins, redeems from death and the devil, and gives eternal salvation to all who believe it, as the words and promise of God declare.

from Matthew 28:16-20

WHAT ARE THESE WORDS AND PROMISES OF GOD?

Where our Lord Christ says in Mark 16, "The one who believes and is baptized will be saved; but the one who does not believe will be condemned."

3. HOW CAN WATER DO SUCH GREAT THINGS?

Clearly the water does not do it, but the word of God, which is with and alongside the water, and faith, which trusts this word of God in the water. For without the word of God the water is plain water and not a baptism, but with the word of God it is a baptism, that is, a grace-filled water of life and a "bath of the new birth in the Holy Spirit," as St. Paul says to Titus in chapter 3, "through the water of rebirth and renewal by the Holy Spirit. This Spirit he poured out on us richly through Jesus Christ our Savior, so that, having been justified by his grace, we might become heirs according to the hope of eternal life. The saying is sure."*

4. WHAT THEN IS THE SIGNIFICANCE OF SUCH A BAPTISM WITH WATER?

It signifies that the old person in us with all sins and evil desires is to be drowned and die through daily sorrow for sin and through repentance, and on the other hand that daily a new person is to come forth and rise up to live before God in righteousness and purity forever.

WHERE IS THIS WRITTEN?

St. Paul says in Romans 6, "We have been buried with Christ by baptism into death, so that, just as Christ was raised from the dead by the glory of the Father, so we too might walk in newness of life."

---

* In Luther's translation of Titus, the last line reads, "This is most certainly true," as in the explanations to the Apostles' Creed and the meaning of Amen in the Lord's Prayer.

HOW PEOPLE ARE TO BE TAUGHT TO CONFESS

WHAT IS CONFESSION?

Confession consists of two parts. One is that we confess our sins. The other is that we receive the absolution, that is, forgiveness, from the pastor as from God himself and by no means doubt but firmly believe that our sins are thereby forgiven before God in heaven.

WHICH SINS IS A PERSON TO CONFESS?

Before God one is to acknowledge the guilt for all sins, even those of which we are not aware, as we do in the Lord's Prayer. However, before the pastor we are to confess only those sins of which we have knowledge and which trouble us.

WHICH SINS ARE THESE?

Here reflect on your place in life in light of the Ten Commandments: whether you are father, mother, son, daughter, master, mistress, servant; whether you have been disobedient, unfaithful, lazy, whether you have harmed anyone by word or deed; whether you have stolen, neglected, wasted, or injured anything.

INDIVIDUAL CONFESSION AND FORGIVENESS*

Confession

The pastor begins:
In the name of the Father,
and of the ✝ Son,
and of the Holy Spirit.
Response: Amen.

OR
Blessed be the holy Trinity,
one God,
who forgives all our sin,
whose mercy endures forever.
Response: Amen.

You have come to make confession before God.
You are free to confess before me,
a pastor in the church of Christ,
sins of which you are aware and which trouble you.

---

* This service of individual confession from *Evangelical Lutheran Worship* (2006) replaces the form used in Luther's day.

The penitent may use the following form or pray in her/his own words.
Merciful God, I confess
that I have sinned in thought, word, and deed,
by what I have done and by what I have left undone.*

*Here the penitent may confess sins that are known and that burden her/
him.***

I repent of all my sins, known and unknown.
I am truly sorry, and I pray for forgiveness.
I firmly intend to amend my life,
and to seek help in mending what is broken.
I ask for strength to turn from sin
and to serve you in newness of life.

*The pastor may engage the penitent in conversation, sharing admonition,
counsel, and comfort from the scriptures. Psalm 51 or Psalm 103 may be
spoken together.*

* An early version of Luther's Small Catechism prepared especially for school children suggests a student might say, "As a student I have not performed my duties diligently. For I have not always done the daily work my teachers have assigned, but have often angered and offended them with my negligence so that they have had to reprimand me because I have not cared about my studies. I also confess that I have spoken and acted indecently, have often become angry with my peers, have often complained about my teachers, and the like."

** At this point Luther reminds us: "If some individuals do not find themselves burdened by these or greater sins, they are not to worry, nor are they to search for or invent further sins and thereby turn confession into torture. Instead mention one or two that you are aware of and let that be enough. If you are aware of no sins at all (which is really quite unlikely), then do not mention any in particular, but instead receive forgiveness on the basis of the general confession that you made to God in the pastor's presence."

Forgiveness

Addressing the penitent, the pastor may lay both hands on the penitent's head.

Cling to this promise: the word of forgiveness I speak to you comes from God.

OR

Name ,
in obedience to the command
of our Lord Jesus Christ,
I forgive you all your sins
in the name of the Father,
and of the ✝ Son,
and of the Holy Spirit.
Response: Amen.

Name ,
by water and the Holy Spirit
God gives you a new birth,
and through the death
and resurrection
of Jesus Christ,
God forgives you all your sins.
Almighty God
strengthen you in all goodness
and keep you in eternal life.
Response: Amen.

The peace of God, which passes all understanding,
keep your heart and your mind in Christ Jesus.
Response: Amen.

The pastor and the penitent may share the greeting of peace.

THE SACRAMENT OF THE ALTAR

1. WHAT IS THE SACRAMENT OF THE ALTAR?

It is the true body and blood of our Lord Jesus Christ under the bread and wine, instituted by Christ himself for us Christians to eat and to drink.

WHERE IS THIS WRITTEN?

The holy evangelists, Matthew, Mark, and Luke, and St. Paul write thus:

In the night in which he was betrayed,
our Lord Jesus took bread,
and gave thanks; broke it,
and gave it to his disciples,
saying: Take and eat;
this is my body, given for you.
Do this for the remembrance of me.

Again, after supper, he took the cup,
gave thanks, and gave it for all to drink,
saying: This cup
is the new covenant* in my blood,
shed for you and for all people
for the forgiveness of sin.
Do this for the remembrance of me.

* Covenant means "promise."

from Matthew 26:26-28

2. WHAT IS THE BENEFIT OF SUCH EATING AND DRINKING?

The words "given for you" and "shed for you for the forgiveness of sin" show us that forgiveness of sin, life, and salvation are given to us in the sacrament through these words, because where there is forgiveness of sins, there is also life and salvation.

3. HOW CAN BODILY EATING AND DRINKING DO SUCH A GREAT THING?

Eating and drinking certainly do not do it, but rather the words that are recorded: "given for you" and "shed for you for the forgiveness of sin." These words, when accompanied by the physical eating and drinking, are the essential thing in the sacrament, and whoever believes these very words has what they declare and state, namely, "forgiveness of sin."

4. WHO, THEN, RECEIVES THIS SACRAMENT WORTHILY?

Fasting and bodily preparation are in fact a fine external discipline, but a person who has faith in these words, "given for you" and "shed for you for the forgiveness of sin," is really worthy and well prepared. However, a person who does not believe these words or doubts them is unworthy and unprepared, because the words "for you" require truly believing hearts.

MORNING AND EVENING BLESSINGS

How the head of the house is to teach the members of the household to say morning and evening blessings.

The Morning Blessing

In the morning, as soon as you get out of bed, you are to make the sign of the holy cross and say:

God the Father, Son, and Holy Spirit watch over me. Amen.

Then, kneeling or standing, say the Apostles' Creed and the Lord's Prayer. If you wish, you may recite this little prayer as well:

I give thanks to you, heavenly Father, through Jesus Christ your dear Son, that you have protected me through the night from all harm and danger. I ask that you would also protect me today from sin and all evil, so that my life and actions may please you. Into your hands I commend myself: my body, my soul, and all that is mine. Let your holy angel be with me, so that the wicked foe may have no power over me. Amen.

After singing a hymn, or whatever else may serve your devotion, you are to go to your work joyfully.

The Evening Blessing

In the evening, when you go to bed, you are to make the sign of the holy cross and say:

God the Father, Son, and Holy Spirit watch over me. Amen.

Then, kneeling or standing, say the Apostles' Creed and the Lord's Prayer. If you wish, you may recite this little prayer as well:

I give thanks to you, heavenly Father, through Jesus Christ your dear Son, that you have graciously protected me today. I ask you to forgive me all my sins, where I have done wrong, and graciously to protect me tonight. Into your hands I commend myself: my body, my soul, and all that is mine. Let your holy angel be with me, so that the wicked foe may have no power over me. Amen.

Then you are to go to sleep quickly and cheerfully.

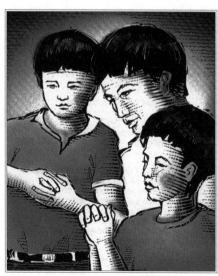

from Psalm 78:1-8

BLESSINGS AT MEALS

How the head of the house is to teach members of the household to offer blessing and thanksgiving at meals.

The Table Blessing

The children and the members of the household are to come devoutly to the table, fold their hands, and recite:

The eyes of all wait upon you, O Lord, and you give them their food in due season. You open your hand and satisfy the desire of every living creature.*

Then they are to recite the Lord's Prayer and the following prayer:

Lord God, heavenly Father, bless us and these your gifts, which we receive from your bountiful goodness, through Jesus Christ our Lord. Amen.

---

* Luther translates this last line from Psalm 145:15-16 "satisfy every living thing with delight," and adds that "delight" means that all animals receive enough to eat to make them joyful and of good cheer, because human worry and greed prevent such delight.

from Psalm 65:9-13

Thanksgiving

Similarly, after eating they should in the same manner fold their hands and recite devoutly:

Give thanks to the Lord, for the Lord is good, for God's mercy endures forever. God provides food for the cattle and for the young ravens when they cry. God is not impressed by the might of a horse, and has no pleasure in the speed of a runner, but finds pleasure in those who fear the Lord, in those who await God's steadfast love.

Then recite the Lord's Prayer and the following prayer:

We give thanks to you, Lord God our Father, through Jesus Christ our Lord for all your benefits, you who live and reign forever. Amen.

THE HOUSEHOLD CHART OF
SOME BIBLE PASSAGES*

Through these verses all kinds of holy orders and walks of life may be admonished, as through lessons particularly pertinent to their office and duty.

FOR BISHOPS, PASTORS, AND PREACHERS**

Now a bishop must be above reproach, married only once, temperate, sensible, respectable, hospitable, an apt teacher, not a drunkard, not violent but gentle, not quarrelsome, and not a lover of money. *1 Timothy 3:2-3*

CONCERNING GOVERNING AUTHORITIES***

Let every person be subject to the governing authorities; for there is no authority except from God, and those authorities that exist have been instituted by God. Therefore whoever resists authority resists what God has appointed, and those who resist will incur judgment. . . . It is the servant of God to execute wrath on the wrongdoer. *Romans 13:1-2, 4b*

* For Martin Luther the death and resurrection of Jesus Christ, to which we are joined in our baptisms, frees us from having to impress God with who we are or what we do. By faith in God's promise in Christ we are free to serve our neighbor, not by escaping from this world to live among "religious" people, but by living our everyday lives. Thus Luther calls daily life a "holy order and estate." He divides life up into three arenas: church, society, and household. This last arena includes what we call the workplace, since in Luther's day most people lived and worked in the same place. He uses Bible verses in what has traditionally been called a "Table of Duties" to suggest how Christians may behave in various "offices" in these three arenas.

Later, Lutherans added material to describe how congregational members ought to treat their pastors and how citizens should behave in society. These biblical references are included in the following notes.

** For the duties of Christians toward their pastors and teachers, see 1 Corinthians 9:14; Galatians 6:6-7; 1 Timothy 5:17-18; 1 Thessalonians 5:12-13; and Hebrews 13:7.

*** For the duties of Christians toward their government, see Matthew 22:21; Romans 13:1, 5-7; 1 Timothy 2:1-2; Titus 3:1; and 1 Peter 2:13-14.

from Deuteronomy 30:11-20

FOR HUSBANDS*

Husbands, in the same way, show consideration for your wives in your life together, paying honor to the woman as the weaker sex, since they too are also heirs of the gracious gift of life—so that nothing may hinder your prayers.
1 Peter 3:7

Husbands, love your wives and never treat them harshly.
Colossians 3:19

FOR WIVES

Wives, in the same way, accept the authority of your husbands, so that, even if some of them do not obey the word, they may be won over without a word by their wives' conduct.... Thus Sarah obeyed Abraham and called him lord. You have become her daughters as long as you do what is good and never let fears alarm you.
1 Peter 3:1, 6

---

* This section for husbands and wives is very difficult for us to understand because in our times the relation between men and women is understood differently than in Luther's day. The following suggestions may help you as you read these passages from the Bible.

In Luther's day everyone, male and female, lived under the authority of someone else. The commoner was under a local lord, the city under the territorial prince, a prince under the emperor. Even the emperor was subject at that time to the parliament and imperial law. To be under someone's authority did not make you less human, nor did it give the one with authority any right to abuse you.

Luther understood that relations between men and women change throughout history. Thus he reminded his own congregation that although women were thought of as property in Old Testament times, such was no longer the case. In our own time most people now support equality between the sexes, as Luther does in explaining the Sixth Commandment.

As a pastor in Wittenberg Luther was very concerned that husbands not mistreat their wives, thus he most likely understood the term "weaker sex" simply in terms of differences in brute strength. He also adds the reference to Colossians 3:19 to exclude any mistreatment of women and includes the last part of 1 Peter 3:6 to make it clear that women should not have to live in fear.

If we were compiling such a chart today, we might include Galatians 3:28 to remind us that Christ God shows no favorites, 1 Corinthians 7:3-4 to show that there should be no sexual exploitation in marriage, and Ephesians 5:21 to remind us that all Christians should server, love, and respect one another.

What remains true is this: each and every Christian has the "office and duty" to love and server their neighbors in whatever arena of life they find themselves.

FOR PARENTS

And, parents, do not provoke your children to anger, but bring them up in the discipline and instruction of the Lord.
based on Ephesians 6:4

FOR CHILDREN

Children, obey your parents in the Lord, for this is right. "Honor your father and mother"—this is the first commandment with a promise: "so that it may be well with you and you may live long on the earth."
Ephesians 6:1-3

FOR EMPLOYEES*

You employees, be obedient to your bosses with respect and coop-eration, with singleness of heart, as to Christ himself; not with service meant only for the eyes, done as people-pleasers, but rather as servants of Christ, so that you do the will of God from the heart [with a good attitude]. Imagine to yourselves that you are serving the Lord and not people, and know that whatever good anyone does, the same will that person receive, whether servant or free.
based on Ephesians 6:5-8

FOR EMPLOYERS

And, bosses, do the same to them. Stop threatening them, for you know that both of you have the same Master in heaven, and with him there is no partiality.
based on Ephesians 6:9

---

* As Luther did in his day, we have altered this section to reflect the economic realities of our day and age, following Luther's own translation of this text.

FOR YOUNG PEOPLE IN GENERAL

In the same way, you who are younger must accept the authority of the elders. And all of you must clothe yourselves with humility in your dealings with one another, for "God opposes the proud, but gives grace to the humble." Humble yourselves therefore under the mighty hand of God, so that he may exalt you in due time.
1 Peter 5:5-6

FOR WIDOWS

The real widow, left alone, has set her hope on God and continues in supplications and prayers night and day; but the widow who lives for pleasure is dead even while she lives.
1 Timothy 5:5-6

FOR ALL IN THE COMMUNITY

The commandments . . . are summed up in this word, "Love your neighbor as yourself."
Romans 13:9

First of all, then, I urge that supplications, prayers, intercessions, and thanksgivings be made for everyone.
1 Timothy 2:1

Let all their lessons learn with care,
So that the household well may fare.

from John 2:1-12

THE MARRIAGE SERVICE*

MARTIN LUTHER'S INTRODUCTION

"So many lands, so many customs," says the common proverb. For this reason, because weddings and the married estate are worldly affairs, it behooves those of us who are pastors and serve the church in no way to order or direct anything regarding marriage, but instead to allow every city and land to continue their own customs that are now in use. Some bring the bride to the church twice, in both the evening and the morning, some only once. Some announce it publicly and publish the banns from the pulpit two or three weeks in advance. All these and similar things I leave to the prince and town council to create and arrange as they want. It is no concern of mine.

However, when people request of us to bless them in front of the church or in the church, to pray over them, or even to marry them, we are obligated to do this.**

Therefore I wanted to offer these words of advice and this order for those who do not know anything better, in case they are inclined to use this common order with us. Others, who can do better (that is, who can do nothing at all and who nevertheless think they know it all), do not need this service of mine, unless they might greatly improve on it and masterfully correct it. They certainly ought to take great care not to follow the same practice as others. A person might think that they had learned something from someone else! Wouldn't that be a shame?

---

* Every edition of the Small Catechism published during Luther's lifetime included the Marriage Booklet. He probably allowed this because in his day almost all households came into existence because of a marriage. Included here are Luther's introduction and, in place of Luther's own marriage service (found in *Luther's Works* 53:110-115), the one from *Evangelical Lutheran Worship* (2006).

** In Luther's day the legal ceremony, consisting of the vows between the man and the woman, took place at the door of the church and the blessing was performed at the altar.

Because up to now people have made such a big display at the consecrations of monks and nuns (even though their estate and existence is an ungodly, human invention without any basis in the Bible) how much more should we honor this godly estate of marriage and bless it, pray for it, and adorn it in an even more glorious manner.*

For, although it is a worldly estate, nevertheless it has God's word on its side and is not a human invention or institution, like the estate of monks and nuns. Therefore it should easily be reckoned a hundred times more spiritual than the monastic estate, which certainly ought to be considered the most worldly and fleshly of all, because it was invented and instituted by flesh and blood and completely out of worldly understanding and reason.

We must also do this in order that the young people may learn to take this estate seriously, to hold it in high esteem as a divine work and command, and not to ridicule it in such outrageous ways with laughing, jeering, and similar levity. This has been common until now, as if it were a joke or child's play to get married or to have a wedding. Those who first instituted the custom of bringing a bride and bridegroom to church surely did not view it as a joke but as a very serious matter. For there is no doubt that they wanted to receive God's blessing and the common prayers and not put on a comedy or a pagan farce.

The ceremony itself makes this clear. For all who desire prayer and blessing from the pastor or bishop indicate thereby—whether or not they say so expressly—to what danger and need they are exposing themselves and how much they need God's blessing and the common prayers for the estate into which they are entering. For we experience every day how much unhappiness the devil causes in the married estate through adultery, unfaithfulness, discord, and all kinds of misery.

* In Luther's day many people wrongly thought that marriage was not as pleasing to God as becoming a monk or nun and imagined that such a "religious" life provided a holy escape from the drudgery and sinfulness of ordinary married life.

The Marriage Service

Gathering

ENTRANCE

*The assembly stands as the ministers and the wedding group enter. Music—
hymn, song, psalm, instrumental music—may accompany the entrance.*

GREETING

The presiding minister and the assembly greet each other.
The grace of our Lord Jesus Christ, the love of God,
and the communion of the Holy Spirit be with you all.
And also with you.

DECLARATION OF INTENTION

*The minister addresses the couple in these or similar words, asking each
person in turn:*
 Name , will you have _name_ to be your *wife/husband*, to live together in the covenant of marriage? Will you love *her/him*, comfort *her/
him*, honor and keep *her/him*, in sickness and in health, and, forsak-
ing all others, be faithful to *her/him* as long as you both shall live?
Response: I will.
The minister may address the assembly in these or similar words.
Will all of you, by God's grace, uphold and care for _name_ and
 name in their life together?
We will.

PRAYER OF THE DAY

The presiding minister leads the following or another prayer of the day.
Let us pray.
Gracious God, you sent your Son Jesus Christ into the world to
reveal your love to all people. Enrich _name_ and _name_ with every
good gift, that their life together may show forth your love; and

grant that at the last we may all celebrate with Christ the marriage feast that has no end; in the name of Jesus Christ our Lord. **Amen**.

Word
READINGS
The assembly is seated. Two or three scripture readings are proclaimed. When the service includes communion, the last is a reading from the gospels. Responses may include a psalm in response to a reading from the Old Testament, a sung acclamation preceding the reading of the gospel, or other appropriate hymns, songs, and psalms.

SERMON
Silence for reflection follows.

HYMN OF THE DAY
A hymn of the day may be sung.

Marriage
VOWS
The couple may join hands. Each promises faithfulness to the other in these or similar words.

I take you, _name_, to be my *wife/husband* from this day forward,
to join with you and share all that is to come,
and I promise to be faithful to you until death parts us.

GIVING OF RINGS
The couple may exchange rings with these or similar words.
Name, I give you this ring as a sign of my love and faithfulness.

ACCLAMATION
The presiding minister addresses the assembly.

Name and _name_ , by their promises before God and in the presence of this assembly, have joined themselves to one another as husband and wife. Those whom God has joined together let no one separate.

Amen. Thanks be to God.

The assembly may offer acclamation with applause. A sung acclamation, hymn, or other music may follow.

Other symbols of marriage may be given or used at this time.

MARRIAGE BLESSING

The couple may kneel. The presiding minister may extend a hand over the couple while praying for God's blessing in the following or similar words.

Most gracious God, we give you thanks for your tender love in sending Jesus Christ to come among us, to be born of a human mother, and to endure the cross for our sake, that we may have abundance of life.

By the power of your Holy Spirit pour out the abundance of your blessing on _name_ and _name_ . Defend them from every enemy. Lead them into all peace. Let your love be a seal upon their hearts, a mantle about their shoulders, and a crown upon their foreheads.

Bless them so that their lives together may bear witness to your love. Bless them in their work and in their companionship; in their sleeping and in their waking; in their joys and in their sorrows; in their life and in their death.

Finally, in your mercy, bring them to that table where your saints feast forever in your heavenly home, through Jesus Christ our Lord, who lives and reigns with you and the Holy Spirit, one God, now and forever.

Amen.

Parents or others may speak additional words of blessing and encouragement at this time.

PRAYERS OF INTERCESSION
The assembly stands. Prayers of intercession for the world and its needs may be prayed.

Each petition may end:
Gracious and faithful God,
hear our prayer.

The presiding minister concludes the prayers, and the assembly responds
Amen.

A service with communion continues with the peace. After the presiding minister greets the assembly, the couple may greet each other with the kiss of peace, and the assembly may greet one another in peace.

A service without communion continues as follows.

LORD'S PRAYER
Our Father in heaven,
 hallowed be your name,
 your kingdom come,
 your will be done, on earth as in heaven.
Give us today our daily bread.
Forgive us our sins
 as we forgive those who sin against us.
Save us from the time of trial
 and deliver us from evil.

**For the kingdom, the power, and the glory are yours,
now and forever. Amen.**

Sending

PEACE

If it has not been included earlier in the service, the greeting of peace may be shared.

The peace of Christ be with you always.

And also with you.

The couple may greet one another with the kiss of peace. All present may greet one another with a gesture of peace, and may say, "Peace be with you," or similar words.

BLESSING

The presiding minister proclaims God's blessing in these or similar words.

The blessed and holy Trinity
make you strong in faith and love,
defend you on every side,
and guide you in truth and peace,
now and forever.

Amen.

DISMISSAL

An assisting minister may send the assembly forth in these or similar words.

Go in peace. Serve the Lord.

Thanks be to God.

A hymn may be sung or instrumental music played as the wedding group and the ministers depart.

from Mark 10:13-16

THE SERVICE OF HOLY BAPTISM*

MARTIN LUTHER'S INTRODUCTION

To all Christian readers:

Grace and peace in Christ our Lord.

Because daily I see and hear with what carelessness and lack of solemnity—to say nothing of out and out levity—people treat the high, holy, and comforting sacrament of baptism for infants, in part caused, I believe, by the fact that those present understand nothing of what is being said and done, I have decided that it is not only helpful but also necessary to conduct the service in the German language. For this reason I have translated those portions that used to be said in Latin in order to begin baptizing in German, so that the sponsors and others present may be all the more aroused to faith and earnest devotion and so that the pastors who baptize have to show more diligence for the sake of the listeners.

Out of a sense of Christian commitment, I appeal to all those who baptize, sponsor infants, or witness a baptism to take to heart

---

* The Marriage service defines the household in relation to God's creation. Holy Baptism defines members of that household in relation to God's grace in Jesus Christ. Included here are Luther's introduction to his own translation of the baptismal service and the service for Holy Baptism from Evangelical Lutheran Worship (using the wording for baptism of infants). The "flood prayer" in this service is adapted from Luther's Baptismal Booklet.

Two important aspects of the Baptismal Booklet are not in this service. First, the ancient service of Holy Baptism that Luther translated from the Latin also included a section in which the pastor meets the baptismal party at the door of the church and commands the devil to leave the child alone. This was not mere superstition, but a clear confession by Luther of the evil in which we all live and of the power of God to use Holy Baptism and its promises to rescue us. It is because of God's act in defeating evil on the cross that we can renounce "all the forces of evil, the devil, and all his empty promises." In Holy Baptism Christ's victory over sin, death, and the devil is applied to us. Luther's conviction that this is true shapes his entire introduction. Second, Luther's service included the reading of Mark 10:13-16, which describes Jesus' blessing of the small children. This helped remind his hearers that Holy Baptism is not something adults do for God, but rather something the Holy Spirit does to us through the water and the Word, no matter what our age, in order that we may trust in God and not in ourselves.

the tremendous work and great solemnity present here. For here in the words of these prayers you hear how plaintively and earnestly the Christian church brings the infant to God, confesses before him with such unchanging, undoubting words that the infant is possessed by the devil and a child of sin and wrath, and so diligently asks for help and grace through baptism, that the infant may become a child of God.

Therefore, you need to consider that it is no joke at all to take action against the devil and not only drive him away from the little child but also hang around its neck such a mighty, lifelong enemy. Thus it is extremely necessary to stand by the poor child with all your heart and with a strong faith and to plead with great devotion that God, in accordance with these prayers, would not only free the child from the devil's power but also strengthen the child, so that the child might resist him valiantly in life and in death. I fear that people turn out so badly after baptism because we have dealt with them in such a cold and casual way and have prayed for them at their baptism without any zeal at all.

Bear in mind, too, that in baptism the external ceremonies are least important, such as blowing under the eyes, making the sign of the cross, putting salt in the mouth or spit and clay in the ears and nose, anointing the breast and shoulders with oil, smearing the head with chrism, putting on the christening robe, placing a burning candle in the child's hand, and whatever else has been added by humans to embellish baptism. For certainly a baptism can occur without any of these things, and they are not the proper devices from which the devil shrinks or flees. He sneers at even greater things than these! Here things must get really serious.

Instead, see to it that you are present there in true faith, that you listen to God's word, and that you pray along earnestly. For wherever the pastors say, "Let us pray," they are exhorting you to pray with them. Moreover, all sponsors and the others present ought to speak along with them the words of their prayers in their hearts to God. For this reason, the pastors should speak these prayers very clearly and slowly, so that the sponsors can hear and understand them and can also pray with the pastors with one mind in their hearts, carrying before God the need of the little child with all earnestness, on the child's behalf setting themselves against the devil with all their strength, and demonstrating that they take seriously what is no joke to the devil.

For this reason it is right and proper not to allow drunken and boorish pastors to baptize nor to select loose people as godparents. Instead fine, moral, serious, upright pastors and godparents ought to be chosen, who can be expected to treat the matter with seriousness and true faith, lest this high sacrament be abandoned to the devil's mockery and dishonor God, who in this sacrament showers upon us the vast and boundless riches of his grace. He himself calls it a "new birth," through which we, being freed from the devil's tyranny and loosed from sin, death, and hell, become children of life, heirs of all God's possessions, God's own children, and brothers and sisters of Christ.

Ah, dear Christians, let us not value and treat this unspeakable gift so half-heartedly. For baptism is our only comfort and doorway to all of God's possessions and to the communion of all the saints. To this end may God help us. Amen.

The Service of Holy Baptism

PRESENTATION

Candidates for baptism, sponsors, and parents gather with the ministers at the font. The assembly may be seated.

The presiding minister may address the assembly in these or similar words.
God, who is rich in mercy and love, gives us a new birth into a living hope through the sacrament of baptism. By water and the Word God delivers us from sin and death and raises us to new life in Jesus Christ. We are united with all the baptized in the one body of Christ, anointed with the gift of the Holy Spirit, and joined in God's mission for the life of the world.

Sponsors for each candidate, in turn, present the candidates.
I present *name* for baptism.

The presiding minister addresses parents or others who bring for baptism children who are not able to answer for themselves.

Called by the Holy Spirit, trusting in the grace and love of God, do you desire to have your children baptized into Christ?
Response: I do.

The presiding minister continues:
As you bring *your children* to receive the gift of baptism, you are entrusted with responsibilities:

    to live with *them* among God's faithful people,
    bring *them* to the word of God and the holy supper,
    teach *them* the Lord's Prayer, the Creed,
    and the Ten Commandments,
    place in *their* hands the holy scriptures,
    and nurture *them* in faith and prayer,
    so that *your children* may learn to trust God,
    proclaim Christ through word and deed,
    care for others and the world God made,
    and work for justice and peace.

Do you promise to help *your children* grow in the Christian faith and life?
Response: I do.

The presiding minister addresses sponsors.
Sponsors, do you promise to nurture *these persons* in the Christian faith as you are empowered by God's Spirit, and to help them live in the covenant of baptism and in communion with the church?
Response: I do.

The presiding minister addresses the assembly.
People of God, do you promise to support ___name/s___ and pray for *them* in *their* new life in Christ?
We do.

The assembly stands.

PROFESSION OF FAITH
The presiding minister addresses candidates for baptism as well as the parents and sponsors of young children. The assembly may join in the responses.
I ask you to profess your faith in Christ Jesus, reject sin, and confess the faith of the church.
Do you renounce the devil and all the forces that defy God?
Response: I renounce them.

Do you renounce the powers of this world that rebel against God?
Response: I renounce them.

Do you renounce the ways of sin that draw you from God?
Response: I renounce them.

The presiding minister addresses the candidates and the assembly.
Do you believe in God the Father?
I believe in God, the Father almighty,
    creator of heaven and earth.

Do you believe in Jesus Christ, the Son of God?
I believe in Jesus Christ, God's only Son, our Lord,
    who was conceived by the Holy Spirit,
    born of the virgin Mary,
    suffered under Pontius Pilate,
    was crucified, died, and was buried;
    he descended to the dead.*
    On the third day he rose again;
    he ascended into heaven,
    he is seated at the right hand of the Father,
    and he will come to judge the living and the dead.

Do you believe in God the Holy Spirit?
I believe in the Holy Spirit,
    the holy catholic church,
    the communion of saints,
    the forgiveness of sins,
    the resurrection of the body,
    and the life everlasting.

THANKSGIVING AT THE FONT
Water may be poured into the font before or during the thanksgiving. At the font, the presiding minister begins the thanksgiving.
The Lord be with you.
And also with you.

---

* Or, "he descended into hell," another translation of this text in widespread use.

Let us give thanks to the Lord our God.
It is right to give our thanks and praise.

We give you thanks, O God, for in the beginning your Spirit moved over the waters and by your Word you created the world, calling forth life in which you took delight. Through the waters of the flood you delivered Noah and his family, and through the sea you led your people Israel from slavery into freedom. At the river your Son was baptized by John and anointed with the Holy Spirit. By the baptism of Jesus' death and resurrection you set us free from the power of sin and death and raise us up to live in you.

Pour out your Holy Spirit, the power of your living Word, that those who are washed in the waters of baptism may be given new life. To you be given honor and praise through Jesus Christ our Lord, in the unity of the Holy Spirit, now and forever.
Amen.

The assembly may be seated.

BAPTISM

The presiding minister baptizes each candidate. The candidate is immersed into the water, or water is poured on the candidate's head, as the presiding minister says:

  Name , I baptize you in the name of the Father,*

The candidate is immersed or water is poured on the candidate's head a second time:

and of the Son,

---

* Or, " Name is baptized in the name of the Father . . ."

The candidate is immersed or water is poured on the candidate's head a third time:
and of the Holy Spirit.
Amen.

After each baptism, the assembly may respond with a sung or spoken alleluia or another acclamation.

OR

Blessed be God,
the source of all life,
the word of salvation,
the spirit of mercy.

You belong to Christ,
in whom you have
been baptized. Alleluia.

Clothed with Christ in baptism, the newly baptized may receive a baptismal garment.
The presiding minister continues:
Let us pray.
We give you thanks, O God, that through water and the Holy Spirit you give your daughters and sons new birth, cleanse them from sin, and raise them to eternal life.
Laying both hands on the head of each of the newly baptized, the minister prays for each:
Sustain _name_ with the gift of your Holy Spirit: the spirit of wisdom and understanding, the spirit of counsel and might, the spirit of knowledge and the fear of the Lord, the spirit of joy in your presence, both now and forever.
Amen.

The presiding minister marks the sign of the cross on the forehead of each of the baptized. Oil prepared for this purpose may be used. As the sign of the cross is made, the minister says:

Name , child of God, you have been sealed by the Holy Spirit and marked with the cross of Christ forever.
Amen.

WELCOME

A lighted candle may be given to each of the newly baptized (to a sponsor of a young child) as a representative of the congregation says:

	OR
Jesus said,	Let your light
I am the light of the world.	so shine before others
Whoever follows me	that they may see
will have the light of life.	your good works
	and glorify your Father
	in heaven.

The ministers and the baptismal group face the assembly. A representative of the congregation leads the assembly in the welcome.
Let us welcome the newly baptized.
We welcome you into the body of Christ
and into the mission we share:
join us in giving thanks and praise to God
and bearing God's creative and redeeming word
to all the world.

Those who have gathered at the font may return to their places. An acclamation, psalm, or hymn may be sung.

The service continues with the prayers of intercession, or, if baptism has taken place in the gathering rite, with the greeting.

LUTHER'S PREFACE TO THE SMALL CATECHISM OF 1529*

Martin Luther, to all faithful and upright pastors and preachers: Grace, mercy, and peace in Jesus Christ our Lord.

The deplorable, wretched deprivation that I recently encountered while I was a visitor has constrained and compelled me to prepare this catechism, or Christian instruction, in such a brief, plain, and simple version. Dear God, what misery I beheld! The ordinary person, especially in the villages, knows absolutely nothing about the Christian faith, and unfortunately many pastors are completely unskilled and incompetent teachers. Yet supposedly they all bear the name Christian, are baptized, and receive the holy sacrament, even though they do not know the Lord's Prayer, the Creed, or the Ten Commandments! As a result they live like simple cattle or irrational pigs and, despite the fact that the gospel has returned, have mastered the fine art of misusing all their freedom.

O you bishops! How are you going to answer to Christ, now that you have so shamefully neglected the people and have not exercised your office for even a single second? May you escape punishment for this! You forbid the cup to the laity in the Lord's supper** and insist on observance of your human laws, while never even bothering to ask whether the people know the Lord's Prayer, the Creed, the Ten Commandments, or a single section of God's word. Shame on you forever!

Therefore, my dear sirs and brothers, who are either pastors or preachers, I beg all of you for God's sake to take up your office boldly, to have pity on your people, who are entrusted to you, and to help us bring the catechism to the people, especially to the young. Moreover, I ask that those unable to do any better take up these

* Here Luther advises pastors on how to teach Christian doctrine and use this book.

** In Luther's day only priests received the wine in the Lord's supper.

charts and versions and read them to the people word for word in the following manner:

In the first place, the preacher should above all take care to avoid changes or variations in the text and version of the Ten Commandments, the Lord's Prayer, the Creed, the sacraments, but instead adopt a single version, stick with it, and always use the same one year after year. For the young and the unlettered people must be taught with a single, fixed text and version. Otherwise, if someone teaches one way now and another way next year—even for the sake of making improvements—the people become quite easily confused, and all the time and effort will go for naught.

The dear church fathers also understood this well. They used one form for the Lord's Prayer, the Creed, and the Ten Commandments. Therefore, we, too, should teach these parts to the young and to people who cannot read in such a way that we neither change a single syllable nor present or recite it differently from one year to the next. Therefore, choose for yourself whatever version you want and stick with it for good. To be sure, when you preach to educated and intelligent people, then you may demonstrate your erudition and discuss these parts with as much complexity and from as many different angles as you can. But with the young people, stick with a fixed, unchanging version and form. To begin with, teach them these parts: the Ten Commandments, the Creed, the Lord's Prayer, etc., following the text word for word, so that they can also repeat it back to you and learn it by heart.

Those who do not want to learn these things—who must be told how they deny Christ and are not Christians—should also not be admitted to the sacrament, should not be sponsors for children at baptism, and should not exercise any aspect of Christian freedom, but instead should simply be sent back home to the pope and his officials and, along with them, to the devil himself. Moreover, their parents and employers ought to deny them food and drink and advise them that the prince is disposed to drive such coarse people out of the country.

Although no one can or should force another person to believe, nevertheless one should insist upon and hold the masses to this: that they know what is right and wrong among those with whom they wish to reside, eat, and earn a living. For example, if people want to live in a particular city, they ought to know and abide by the laws of the city whose protection they enjoy, no matter whether they believe or are at heart scoundrels and villains.

In the second place, once the people have learned the text well, then teach them to understand it, too, so that they know what it means. Take up again the form offered in these charts or some other short form that you may prefer. Then adhere to it without changing a single syllable, just as was stated above regarding the text. Moreover, allow yourself ample time for it, because you need not take up all the parts at once but may instead handle them one at a time. After the people understand the First Commandment well, then take up the Second, and so on. Otherwise they will be so overwhelmed that they will hardly remember a single thing.

In the third place, after you have taught the people a short catechism like this one, then take up a longer catechism and impart to them a richer and fuller understanding. Using such a catechism, explain each individual commandment, petition, or part with its various works, benefits and blessings, harm and danger, as you find treated at length in so many booklets. In particular, put the greatest stress on that commandment or part where your people experience the greatest need. For example, you must strongly emphasize the Seventh Commandment, dealing with stealing, to artisans and shopkeepers and even to farmers and household workers, because rampant among such people are all kinds of dishonesty and thievery. Likewise, you must emphasize the Fourth Commandment to children and the common people, so that they are orderly, faithful, obedient, and peaceful. Always adduce many examples from the scriptures where God either punished or blessed such people.

In particular, at this point also urge governing authorities and parents to rule well and to send their children to school. Point out how they are obliged to do so and what a damnable sin they commit if they do not, for thereby, as the worst enemies of God and humanity, they overthrow and lay waste both the kingdom of God and the kingdom of the world. Explain very clearly what kind of horrible damage they do when they do not help to train children as pastors, preachers, civil servants, etc., and tell them that God will punish them dreadfully for this. For in our day and age it is necessary to preach about these things. The extent to which parents and governing authorities are now sinning in these matters defies description. The devil, too, intends to do something horrible in all this.

Finally, because the tyranny of the pope* has been abolished, people no longer want to receive the sacrament [of the altar], and they treat it with contempt. This, too, needs to be stressed, while keeping in mind that we should not compel anyone to believe or to receive the sacrament and should not fix any law or time or place for it.** Instead, we should preach in such a way that the people make themselves come without our law and just plain compel us pastors to administer the sacrament to them. This can be done by telling them: You have to worry that whoever does not desire or receive the sacrament at the very least around four times a year despises the sacrament and is no Christian, just as anyone who does not listen to or believe the gospel is no Christian. For Christ did not say, "Omit this," or "Despise this," but instead, "Do this, as often as you drink it . . ." He really wants it to be done and not completely omitted or despised. "Do this," he says.

---

* Luther's strong language reflects his ongoing struggle with the institutional church of his day.

** In Luther's day all Christians had to commune between Easter and ten days after Pentecost.

Those who do not hold the sacrament in high esteem indicate that they have no sin, no flesh, no devil, no world, no death, no dangers, no hell. That is, they *believe* they have none of these things, although they are up to their ears in them and belong to the devil twice over. On the other hand, they indicate that they need no grace, no life, no paradise, no heaven, no Christ, no God, nor any other good thing. For if they believed that they had so much evil and needed so much good, they would not neglect the sacrament, in which help against such evil is provided and in which so much good is given. It would not be necessary to compel them with any law to receive the sacrament. Instead, they would come on their own, rushing and running to it; they would compel themselves to come and would insist that you give them the sacrament.

For these reasons you do not need to make any law concerning this, as the pope did. Only emphasize clearly the benefit and the harm, the need and the blessing, the danger and the salvation in this sacrament. Then they will doubtless come on their own without any compulsion. If they do not come, give up on them and tell them that those who do not pay attention to or feel their great need and God's gracious help belong to the devil. However, if you either do not urge such participation or make it into a law or poison, then it is your fault if they despise the sacrament. How can they help but neglect it, if you sleep and remain silent?

Therefore, pastors and preachers, take note! Our office has now become a completely different one than it was under the pope. It has now become serious and salutary. Thus, it now involves much toil and work, many dangers and attacks, and in addition little reward or gratitude in the world. But Christ himself will be our reward, so long as we labor faithfully. May the Father of all grace grant it, to whom be praise and thanks in eternity through Christ, our Lord. Amen.